Blue in this Country

OTHER BOOKS
BY ZOË LANDALE

Rain is Full of Ghosts (River Books, 2000) novel

Burning Stone (Ronsdale, 1995) poetry

Colour of Winter Air (Sono Nis, 1991) poetry

Shop Talk, editor (Pulp Press, 1985) poetry

Harvest of Salmon (Hancock House, 1976) non-fiction

February 1, 2001

Blue in this
Country

p o e m s

*For Calvin with
love at our SIWU
reunion @ Green
College*

Zoë Landale

Zoë

RONSDALE PRESS

RONSDALE PRESS
3350 West 21st Avenue
Vancouver, B.C., Canada
V6S 1G7

Set in New Baskerville: 11 pt on 13.5
Typesetting: Julie Cochrane
Printing: Hignell Printing, Winnipeg, Manitoba
Cover Art: Pnina Granirer, *Blue Mountain*, 30" x 22", acrylic on paper
Cover Design: Julie Cochrane
Back Cover Author Photo: Boomer Jerritt

Ronsdale Press wishes to thank the Canada Council for the Arts, the Government of Canada through the Book Publishing Industry Development Program (BPIDP), and the Province of British Columbia through the British Columbia Arts Council for their support of its publishing program.

CANADIAN CATALOGUING IN PUBLICATION DATA

Landale, Zoë, 1952–
   Blue in this country

   Poems.
   ISBN 0-921870-81-7

   I. Title.
PS8573.A5315B58 2001   C811'.54   C00-911227-8
PR9199.3.L294B58 2001

CONTENTS

For my aunt,
Susette Simmins

ACKNOWLEDGEMENTS

Thanks to the editors of the following magazines and anthologies who published poems in this book: *The New Quarterly, Canadian Literature, Arc, the literary hot girls review* (US), *Event, TickleAce, american goat* (US), *Contemporary Verse 2, Pottersfield Portfolio, Grail: An Ecumenical Journal, Dandelion, Prairie Fire, Grain, Undertow, The Wascana Review, Quarter Moon, Other Voices, Whetstone, Prism international, Vintage '92, North Coast Collection.*

"Miracle" was a finalist in the 1994 Stephen Leacock Poetry Awards.

"David and His Father at Calgary Airport" won second prize in the 1995 Stephen Leacock Poetry Awards.

"Waiting for the Word in a Bone-White Garden" was awarded first prize for a poem published by the Canadian Church Press in 1997.

"Mother of Lights" was awarded first prize for a poem published by the Canadian Church Press in 1998.

Special thanks to George McWhirter

– ONE –

Creed

I believe in the spiritual rootedness
of mountains, that they extend
far beyond the blue, treed slopes we recognize,

that the dead know streams
not as we see them, burbling between
banks of fern and horsetail
but weightless as a cello concerto,
fragrant as strawberries.

I believe the way to at-one-ment
is to become water,
the idea behind molecules
sliding cool as summer morning
before the sun burns off mist
from the dawn-grey hills.

Daily, we swirl over our ordinary shoulders
the cloak of prophecy
worn
with becoming.

The Man with the Split Thumb

Skin speaks a language
of anguish
that is circular
drives in at itself.
Rashes
small cracks, swellings
I finger like disastrous miracles:
one touch
and I am converted painfully
to the testimony of sense.

Skin says in broken consonants:
       I hurt
       I am open
flesh all the way to the tendons
dark red showing
along pulled-back lips.

Skin articulates
all I cannot.

Skin is too noisy.
I wish for myself silent
beauty, hands that do not weep lymph;
for the man
with the split thumb
a dialect less vulnerable
than blood.

Yellow

My responsibility is to follow the yellow line
between wood and flesh
to refuse the impact.
Yellow, danger, the police tape
around the scene
of an accident or murderous blow:
whichever, the body fell
to the left
into the five foot green ditch
beside the golf course.
The family mourns
with a roughly made cross
marking the spot,
white cherry blossom already wilting
in the unseasonable April heat.

Unreasonable, the demand to be clubbed
again and again.
Isn't this what's exacted though,
the sudden strike
from behind
just when a person thinks she has mastered
the cool art of pushing limbs
through the heavy day?

As if happiness demands its opposite,
as if day lies on its back and cries out
to be covered by night,
annihilation is publicly gleeful,

goes about with a face like a bull terrier,
sports a bloody snout,
makes disgusting slurping noises
of appreciation
every time someone dies.

The raising up,
the coming down
of terror.

Surely yellow tape will save
some secret corner
that remembers the innocence
of blazing delphiniums
the blue so strong I could swing a world from it.
Yellow will shield the blue,
won't it,
from the coming of the club,
the *whissh* of tearing air?

Yellow will preserve us all,
or so I believe.

Yellow is the structure
I can hastily put between me
and the blow.
My responsibility is to remember
yellow
the exact shade of its safety,
the texture
of yellow's terrifyingly thin
protective line.

Shelter

Terror has made me small.
I shelter under the wing
of the wind,
under the Japanese painted fern.
Its dry ridge of spine
holds me safe
from the edge.

On the undersides,
blessings fine as feathers
comfort skin.

Sanctification
of the miniature.

Safety if I scrunch small enough
if I hang onto the sweet heat
that spreads the cupped wing.

Cusp of the wind.
I dangle on its black lip
poised,
hope for the swell
of a miracle.
At any moment now,
the fern's blanket will allow my body
to warm.
I will sleep,
I will not roll out
from under its silver fringe.

Swan

It is easier to desire lightning
than to forswear it

electricity dancing
the vivid vertebrae white

as the mouths of tiny
night-flying insects
scribing their dance

weightless as ash

in soft air.

Anyone can say *Strike me
dead*

and mean it, it is the pale flare
of light behind the curtains

morning after morning

that takes all I have
to rise and face.

Often I am awkward as a swan
with fury.

Where are the dreams
I had only moments before,

those tender green hopes

I like to let drape
lavishly on either side of my beak?

It causes less commotion to store
the bulbous dry
un-lit hours
lined up
than to speak my disappointment.

I am a hungry swan, perhaps,
but not stupid

though I look at summer lightning,
those succulent white-blue arcs
of annihilation,

with greed

and am ashamed.

Housewifery

I have allowed my days
to grow swollen
as cauliflowers.
They dangle like distorted skulls
at the end of each arm.

There's a trick to handling these
white days
I haven't yet found.

Too many details:
graininess of laundry,
the kitchen floor muddy
again.
I want my rooms
bare as a Japanese house,
elegant as bone.
As clean.
My family will be home at any moment.
They will mess things up.
Again.
I am prepared for the chaos they trail
in their wake,
earth in the grooves of their shoes.
The baby with her sharp intakes
of delight, of *Ooo* as she grabs at drawers.

Only part of me
wants to scour my way
to a closed universe,
a house where gleaming skulls
will smile from the mantel
dustless forever.

In the Garden, Take Two

Eve is dreaming a woman
alone in an orchard.
The smell of apples reminds her
she is not milk-white and glistening
marble in the cool blue of evening,
fragrance of approaching dew
long grasses
heavy seed heads drooping.

Strange for sleep to be
so detailed,
pervasive with the scent
of apples.

Eve's still point is grief
around which she swings, violet,
sharp as comprehension,
as if someone had told her
a sister had died, a terrible bloom
unfolding.

*

no
nothing
no thing
not what she will become
Not who she thought she was

Leaves waver, green hands appalled
at revelation.
All through the smell of apples
she has known it was coming,

this constriction of vision
and anguish
for the weak one she will imagine herself
to be, someday.

Eve is alone in the orchard
dreaming a woman
with a silver spoon who will wake her
from the scent of apples.

Stars are rents. The cosmos peeks
through, burning.
Evening echoes blue
tender as a mother,
the lulling dark arms of branches.

Waiting for the Word in a Bone-White Garden

My father feels his life has been
one white sorrow after another,
wings that tear
as soon as formed.
He has lived with sadness
until its cut
is familiar, almost unnoticed
like the first stroke
from a sharp boning
knife.

His brilliant father
who got him drunk
when he
was five years old.
No point in touching
the why.

His dead wish him well.
My father imagines them loving him
delicately
fiercely as metal
sliding
through skin.

He has flown
and fallen.
He expects no more.
Life is an open blade
that the pressure of time
holds to his wings.

Once, the creator spoke to him
over the rubble of Europe, as
he lay exhausted in the back of an
army truck.
He said no.

Twice more
this warmth behind the universe has spoken,
electrifying him with the conviction
of some deeper reason
behind loss.

Now my father calls himself old.
The universe is silent,
and sadness a white garden
he moves through.
He tries
not to get irritable.

He speaks to this stilled
echo,
rubs nubs on his shoulders
where something large
and lovely as a striped sail once grew.
They itch.

His dead answer
with the sounds
of tiny bells.
They have failed
to protect him.
It is not for them my father listens
but the Word which will make sense
of his sorrow
bind white
into a shape that soars with
wild
feathered joy.

Cat

for Kii

All winter long I expected
something to bloom from the cat's grave
a remarkable flower, perhaps
as sinuous and exaggerated as he was,

stalk like a Celtic cross, the elegant spiral
his chocolate tail made against his creamy flank
one and a half times the length of any tail I ever
saw before, Siamese show stock.

All winter I glanced at his grave
every time I went in the front door
said hello, knowing well what I greeted
was not him, really

but the essence of cat
and it's this idea I want to flower,
more baroque than pink *nerines*
fresher-smelling than even daffodils.

All winter that mound of earth has been barren
of anything but a few blades of grass and grief
but this morning
a memory arrives, cool as mint,

I wake feeling him draped
around my neck, his weight and
elegance, cat as fur scarf.
This is balm.

All winter I have thought of him
as *that impossible cat*, who hid from any but the three
he lived with, whose idea of friendliness
was to go into the middle of the room and scream for a pat

who woke up the household regularly,
cat as foghorn, an exaggeration of course,
but everything about him was too intense
except for his adoration of me, which was just fine.

All winter I have been glad
we were able to put up the bird feeder again.
That cat used to sit in the leafless pear tree
for hours, perfectly visible, and incredibly

successful at batting rosy house finches from branches
or on the wing, and robins, red-winged blackbirds,
regardless of his collar and silvery, useless bell
until we took the feeder down.

All winter long I have known my cat
would not come back again as an amaryllis
or a red trumpet of any kind
but I kept hoping

and now I will settle, gratefully, for the lithe feel of him
around my neck, that perfect, delighted confidence
as I tossed him in the air
and he curled to meet my shoulders, purring.

Infinity is the Sudden Lilt

Infinity is a door in grey wood,
opening.
It's right the way
the door angles
from bevelled siding.
Though it surprises me
to find this extra entrance
in my own house,
I am glad to pass through.

Enough horsing around
with the horizontal.

Infinity is the sudden lilt
of the vertical.

If anyone needed sustaining
it's me,
this mild day of one more
crisis.
The charm of snowdrops and crocus
only buzzes my eyes,
doesn't sink in.

Infinity is the sudden turning
in wood
when all the molecules stand to attention.
Point, say:
*This.   This is where the sweetness
of afternoon comes from.
Follow,*
and I go

knowing
the papery beauty
of *helleborus,* Easter roses,
purple and white,
the solidity of what beckons
is an armful of more than space
by the back stairs
cold freshness of February daphne,
twigs pink, awhirl with bloom.

I am the winter
opening.

Infinity is the gap
in grey,
that praising,
prising,
I continually
step through.

David and his Father
at Calgary Airport

David is webbing the world,
invisibly,
casting out from his father
who sits in a black plastic chair
in the Calgary airport.
His father watches his sixteen-month-old son
with the slight, crucified smile
of a man
unable to believe
his own happiness.

David, cheeks red-chapped,
rocks
as he walks the lines
out from his father's bearded
sanctuary.
Today he wears his green jumpsuit,
with one red arm, one blue.
He moves with the solemn walk
of the fat-diapered.
Fifty feet away and David
turns. Back.

His father's heart is a spiked fish
in his chest,
flopping.
The pure gaze of his boy.
The sharp *Aa* of joy that David gives
on finding
that same face
safe at the centre

again.
Almost all the way
back, the boy turns
in a different direction.
The father lets him
go.

David is weaving.
The word is not one he knows,
not *hot* nor *head* nor *shoe,*
but the imperative is there, to tread
certainty through his feet
into this strange place
with the people, the noise,
the slippery tile floor.

David's mouth is open.
He stagger-runs into the sparkly
air, making pathways.
What leads away
leads back, that is the delight
that keeps him stomping
and balanced
at the end of the delicate rotation
about his father,
the axis.
Aa, David shouts when his father keeps
reappearing.

The father laughs, just a little,
as his son
keeps reeling him in.

In the Schoolyard

Moms throw love after their children
who disappear as fast as possible
through the heavy double doors
behind the gym.
I love you, honey,
a woman with straight brown hair to her waist
calls after her seven-year-old boy
who doesn't look back
doesn't smile.

The bell has rung.

Wrung me into silence
seeing all these women
loving their children with hasty spears
of tenderness.
Holding hands with morning-clean kids,
speeding their way to classrooms
with wriggled-away-from kisses
green and yellow and black packsacks changing hands.

A hundred feet before the doors
my daughter, a whole week into Grade One, says
Stay here, mummy
and sets off running.
I lean against a metal pillar, watch her red tights
flash.
She glances back, once,
to see if I am still there.

I am here, child.
Here for as long as it takes
standing in the chilly September sun
with the other mothers, some who try in vain
for hugs
and one father, who straddles his bicycle
still watching his son
with the same mildly exasperated
expression of adoration
the rest of us wear pinned through our hearts.

Miracle

Today my daughter is a miracle
rushing into the huge white sky
that is the playing field tipped with snow
up to the blanched horizon.

What astonishes is the brightness of her colours;
never before have I seen the sweetness
of purple
the intense bloom of it so clearly

as her purple coat, purple hat with two
pink pompoms
purple mitts luminous as tropical birds at the ends
of her swinging arms.

My child's legs
have the thin beauty of a flamingo's
pink tights in pink snow boots
thudding confidently up the path to school.

She is alone in the snowy world, this wondrous
child, one minute late and running
when she unexpectedly turns, flaps her purple and pink
    lunch kit
at me in gleeful acknowledgement

of something, my dumbfoundedness
from the car, perhaps,
or merely saying hello and goodbye
from the wide white rim of morning.

Communion

Wind bends tall cottonwoods on the island
so silver backs of their leaves show,
turn up like the hands of painted saints
pointed in prayer.

I am happy
this good strong emotion
still runs green and deep
to the sea.
I had thought
all that was left

dry river-run stone.

I am happy
to submerge myself
in peace that flows like a river.
I am happy
to be green,
sniff the balsamic adoration of cottonwoods
watch the closer domestic ecstasy
of two robins in the crabapple
mate
quick
as pebbles rolling in the flood-tide.

Here the wind is fragrant
at the still point
of the turning day.

– T W O –

Running

1

What I am running from
breathless in clean morning sun
is the way he is an eiderdown
to me.
Night after night
my body must pretend it is flannel;
we cuddle
and cannot close
the salt gulf of bed.

Woman as white magnolia soap.

Down into the abyss of sleep
we go together.
Some wakeful body part of me
floats along dark's surface
crooning
as a child might
in a strange house.

2

What I am running toward
are green eyes
his unshaven face that Sunday morning
how he caught me to him
by the kitchen sink
ran his hands over

me, the great warm whoosh
of desire
blossoming pink
between us.

3

What I am running from
is leaving.
I want to live in sun-splashed woods
in a tiny whorled house
of clapboard,
become aromatic and sexless
as cedar,
grow *achillea* with golden eyes:
it dries well.

4

In all my running
I would like a place
to rest.
The gravel beneath my thick
shoes is angry as breaking waves.
Thoughts are petrels, they spray up,
cannot settle.
I wish
hope
could come up suddenly emerald
as the high hump of Solander Island rises
off the West Coast
of Vancouver Island.
Without hope

I am a boat shattering
on the reef of green eyes,
consolation of them,
dread at impact.

(Salt water sprays between
stove-in planks.
Seams of light bloom between splintered wood
and no running will warm that sudden silver
influx of ocean
nor make it bloom.)

Vows

I do not get over
my habit of loyalty.
I pull on
your terror.
You sleep without dreaming
of the fear.
I wear it next to my skin,
and long silver stars through my lobes.
They itch and burn.

I am too old to believe
faithfulness will transform
me into saint
or princess
but that feudal alignment
sparkles along my napped fabric,
the gleam
of a cross.
Precious metal.

Give me a kiss then,
a medal
of thanks.
Tell me the tug of obligation
is worth all the times
I wake and pray
and the comfort of spirit,
its infinite bowl,
gives right of way to dawn.
The ceiling is eight feet from the floor
blank
and smells of fresh paint.

The amnesia of morning.
What it costs me
to love
when the world is sliced by the sharp edges
of stars.

The Vasectomy

I have been much in need
of comfort lately,
my body light as a whelk shell
whorled, sliding in the surf line,
and only sand at home.

So, I abrade —
dogfish skin does too
and the rubbed lip of beaches on green glass
spat out, left for the tide
to suck and mourn.

Never again to feel
the sting of milk
coming down in breasts stiff as wood —
a singular self,
not festooned with child.

I shall have to take my body for walks
encourage it to play in the seaweed,
snuffle up softness of beach air,
good body, so obedient, it always comes
when called.

My husband takes bagged baby clothes,
the stroller it took so long to pay for
to the shelter for battered women.
Our five-year-old teases for a sister
and I am weightless, a long salt cadence.

End of the Road

Grey on the map, a dragged-out heart. I say into the wind, I am not this emptiness. June wind is damp, cold enough to make ears ache. Estuary is head-high with grass, ripples like a fine horse's coat, sleek with growth. Evening primrose, milky yellow exclamation marks.

The barrenness of waiting.

Something builds, urgent. Low rumble of a train at Roberts Bank, engine vibrating across the flat miles. Stones underfoot, fine dust of striding sifts over my running shoes, puffy white with turquoise and pink trim.

All that needs to be done is tumble head-first into the well of infinity.

Potatoes planted in rows, green corduroy stripes run back to the field's beginning. Between the dike and the sea, the wide sky, hung with grey clouds and the painted rim of mountains, blue as memory. Sacred blue. White for renunciation. Is this what I wait for, the grace to say it doesn't matter?

I wish for more blooms. Last time there was wild iris, yellow as buttercup. Now there is pink clover. A weed with arms red and papery as bougainvillaea, leaves like dock but flushed with red. Purple vetch. Queen's Ann's lace. The colours grow isolated in tiny patches. What I see is green shivering, the sky like rain.

Something finished, perfect as paper. Blank. Walk with
a smile at all times in case someone might be looking.
Endurance, an under-rated virtue. The high dike curves
to the shabby farm, though why so neglected I cannot
understand, this delta land surpassingly rich. A convocation
of gulls where shore and sea touch. White droplets against
salt pewter.

Today is the grey time when I implore strength. I am not this
desolation, I say into the wind. On the map, a dragged-out
heart. Waiting.

Oatmeal Cookies

Cinnamon, brown
sugar. Butter.
      These are defences
      I have chosen.
      I employ them with precision,
wooden spoon, the yellow radiance
the plastic mixing bowl makes against
the white counter.
      No more children.
      I will not think that.
Heat from the oven.

      No rosemary, that's for
      remembrance.

Sweet spices, that's what I'm after
this raw winter morning,
      the way
      my brother's sixteen-month-old child
      filled his arms:
      completeness of motion, the boy in constant
      scrambling delight against his father's chest.
      The tatami room at the restaurant,
      the child's golden head.
      He eats California rolls,
      bangs on walls, beams
      at his own noise.

I beat in egg, add
vanilla, mix in
      all the dry ingredients.
      — *Gentle, gentle,* how I unclenched
      the boy's hands from my eight-year-old's hair —

I slide the first batch
of cookies
into the oven.
The smell of baking eases the raw clutch of panic.
      The boy in his father's arms
      gurgling,
      my kind, pregnant sister-in-law,
      are still seated across from me,
      figures in a gold-stroked
      Japanese screen.
      The tatami room gradually becomes awash
    with possibilities.

      The openings are there,
      mesh spangled with
    cheeriness
      in the dreary December rain.

The boy breaks free from his father. My sister-in-law laughs.

In my kitchen, I stay with warmth.
I refuse to believe in anything
but the sure way
my life fills up with goodness,
runs over.
All that love. My cookies,
the smell of cinnamon rich
in loosening air.

My Mother & the Moon

My mother has swallowed silence
drunk it down like the moon
white in her cup.

After decades, silence has grown large
is comfortable,
nestles in my mother's throat.

There, silence whispers its tiny song
the colour of a wren in winter alder twigs:
dun on brown. The music of camouflage.

At seventy-eight, my mother cannot tell us how she is.
She says she *is better now.* Better than falling
on ice, than nearly tumbling on stairs.

It is silence we have to ask about her, really,
and it knows more than to leave the place
where it is so round, so perfectly blocks

my mother's pain from escaping. It wants no tell-tale
whimpers that mean reddened feathers: *Look here* or stories
of how our mother accuses herself, she of the patience

that roots in the pre-Cambrian shield. Mother believes the best
of her family. She wants wishes to be early stars,
there for the blessing of her son and daughters.

But the moon, the moon. My mother drank it back
when her words were fire and easily called upon to scorch the
    guilty.
Maybe it was to cool the ache

in her tired throat, maybe it was water when she was thirsty.
Certainly her mother taught her the value of white,
how it smooths the unruly emotions

into a landscape of tolerance.
All that untidy brush soothed with snow,
one colour and one shape, dazzling, horizontal.

You keep your secrets, my grandmother commanded
her, *in the family. Never tell.* And my mother lifted that cup,
swirled the moon about in cold well water, drank.

She found silence
anaesthetized nicely. Her father, accidentally shot
on the porch by a drinking buddy.

Full military honours at his funeral. The small-town
Ontario street lined with mourners, his casket carried
high on the shoulders of Masonic brothers

and Mother fourteen then, desperate for white, pulling
it from the air around her, the stiff spine of my unbending
grandmother. Clouds the shape of running dogs.

White is the colour of calm.
White would never parade before strangers the shame
of her sister at sixteen, sloe-eyed and sloping

off with every male available. White kept that locked down
under its bed of winter pearl. When her sister married safely
two years later, my mother and her mother

exchanged significant glances. No words, birds that could
    betray
too easily, flutter out anytime in church or living room.
And white was flattered that demand for ice was so high.

The moon was in its element then, all slip
and miss of meaning. Shadows and the smell
of lilac on warm spring nights. The misdirection of white.

2

This past Christmas. My mother twists on her couch.
What's the matter? I ask.
She straightens. *Just a little tired.*

I extract from her, finally, that her back hurts. I rub it.
My mother makes smothered noises, almost cries.
The moon is laughing. *Soo much better,* my mother keeps

saying. Her vowels drawn into long quavers
that make tears start for me: I stop them;
I am my mother's daughter enough for that.

I wish I could make things better.
Always there's guilt and I've never known why;
a feeling I had too much and she too little.

Maybe it's the words, how my mother keeps reaching
for them, unable to describe just the colour she wants
in the sunset, the tenderness of leaves that eludes her.

And I live in a nest of words, warmed and guarded;
they're like dogs held to the heart of the family
moving confidently around the house, tails wagging

noses alert to domestic air. Waiting for handouts or pats;
the praise they know is their due.
Good words, alert for their opportunity to move in.

My mother and the moon know nothing of this camaraderie.
The silence this Christmas has intensified,
is cool and poised as air around the rim of a well,

shaded with ferns, and even on a summer's day,
there's the shock of a world drawn apart unto itself —
fall in July. It speaks of moisture and north, the waning

of light. And Mother, I am afraid for you. Afraid of the moon,
its gelid calm; how so little comes out
that you want. How your heart lurches as you try

and your mouth is empty and the moon
sings its private song in your full throat. Again. You turn
by the stairs, leaving unsaid what you want to say, and grumble

you will not get dressed for the holiday dinner.
Our family secrets are safe with you.
You keep your tense white bargain.

Red Tulips

1

The astonishing geometry of pain,
the green centeredness of spent tulip heads
in my hand,
the way you turn from me
without a glance
stride to the truck
gleaming under shadows of the hazel.

The remains of the tulips
are three-sided, cool
to touch
and utterly fail to console
with their form.

As if she were a woman
you could not resist,
you yield fiercely
to black despair.
Your hands are pinioned under her much smaller,
harder ones
as if she rode you
while you strove and strove
to buck out from under
and died.
I see you die as you go;
your eyes full of angry energy
miles from the white azalea by your feet.

I would not let you drive but
you have our daughter
in the truck.
For her, you will return
undamaged
to the garden,
the trembling leaves.

2

In preference to
your face, compliant
with despondency, I look at the
snapped-off tulip heads.

Each tulip has three green frills
at its tip,
beguilingly curved,
doubled-edged.
I think of an ornamental penis.
Slightly paler than the stalk
the frills are edged with fine damp
velvet, barely seen.
They are mad and jaunty things I hold —
another tiny triangle twists in the
curves of the other —
staring as if I would open it like scrying glass,
the glass of my heart, yours,
the world's.
Seed pods.

Red-petalled
and bold they were,
common hardy Darwins
that keep appearing
year after year.
I like those gaudy survivors
that thrive in bands.
All over the garden are solitary tulips,
lily-flowered
and showy as the points and spires
of columbines.
Another year or so
and those exotics will be like Shakers,
too pure for this sphere.

3

Wild *scylla hyacinthoides* flaunt
blue stirrings
through the garden.
Tomorrow will be May.
The red blooms are all gone, my dear,
and every morning
the sky comes again
outside the curtained windows
in a swing of white light.
Your battle with despair I cannot win
or even fight
for you.
All I can say
is the days dangle

us like string
and you, you are woven
to me
with the sheen of tulips,
the boisterous brown hair
of our daughter,
the radiance
of this ordinary garden,
where each year
we at least stand together.

Prayer for My Husband

Day and leaves have overtaken the lights.
Flood tide of elder, maple, thimbleberry
instead of tugboats
reduced to red and green
against the purring dark night.
The white *I am towing* light at the stern,
a purposeful flower.

I have stopped at the viewpoint
where I retreated
thirteen years ago
when we fought.

It is June, mild.
Traffic rushes by into air that is
always the same,
wheels the "o" of hope
clicking on the rough road.

A single wild rose
a prayer, pink:
see, there is order
if only we will accept it.
It is the size of stars
and beyond our sight.
We are
safe.

Across the city, I want to extend
the rose to you, say
Here,
this is the axis,
temporarily.
Watch the lovely world turn
planted in balance.

Flight No 272,
Vancouver to New York

I stare at the brown bones
of the country beneath,
and think of you.
Swirled around empty air,
a loop of cloud slides by.
Intricate mesh, the shawl
our daughter still wears
to play princess. She is seven.
Her great-aunt crocheted
the white acrylic for her at birth.

At thirty-seven thousand feet
Washington is a dry
articulation
of stilled mountains.
High lakes are rimmed
with ice.
The book that you were enjoying
and gave me to take
is open on my lap.
You have not finished yet.
In six days I will bring it back,
bury my face in the tender
skin of your neck.
For now, the book rests
on my knee,
light as a hand-made shawl,
binding as a kiss
I carry with me
across the hours of continent.

U-Pick

The berries burn
against blue sky. I cannot believe
their red.
It is as though all my years have spun
and stopped at this moment
bent above the strawberry plants
holding a ripe heart
crouched under the wind-burnished immensity
of horizon.

I know how to tell when they're good,
my daughter says,
leaping between rows.
The stems make a little noise when you pick them.
The two of us make squeaky snaps
with the berries' green strings.
In the ditch between two fields —
how rolled flat the world is, how the sky
looms —
a frog sends out shoots
of sound, ragged as bracken.

The berries blaze
so I pull down my sunglasses to check,
yes, they really are the urgent shade
they seemed.

It is Father's Day. I am picking a bucket
full for strawberry shortcake.
The north-westerly flips
hair in my face
so I peer through a mane
at fire.
My eight-year-old runs down the rows,
snatching berries, laughing,
a torrent
in a too-large T-shirt.
Picking for her is done standing,
a pour of movement between the fragrant electric berries,
stained fingers and mouth.

The berries burn.
I think of the man at home
and smile,
the way his green eyes will lift to mine.
Today I am bringing home
incandescence
to eat with cream.

The Electric Animal

The electric animal between us
is not sex
though that fleet sizzle
of tension
invites comparison.
The animal is cobalt and neon blue.
It crackles in the quiet kitchen.

The charge of eyes, held,
makes me want you
like the first time though
the animal knows nothing of hazel eyes or green;
is abysmally ignorant
of the aphrodisiac qualities of milky tea.

We stand, hugging each other.
Our personal lines of dark,
where the energies roll
in a lacing of arms,
fold the stored force and ground.

I feel how thin you are suddenly.
The overhead lights
shine on the white skin
of your chest and through;
you turn translucent.

Age wears us fine
as paper, crinkles us.

The electric animal
is a harsh companion.
Between us, we have sheltered it unwittingly.
Mangy, snapping, it flits indoors, then hides
when heads are turned.
We know the feel of it now,
that tension we might almost miss
if it were gone. The clench
of stomach muscles, the awakening
at three a.m. Pure
terror, dazzling in its blue
insistence upon itself, the way
it fills up whole rooms
with geometric iterations of fear.

- THREE -

Pulling Down Revelations

I live in spaces the texture of egg shell,
brown ovals balanced
on my uneven kitchen counter
just so.
Between performances in the red
and white tent outside,
I am glad of a cup of tea.
Treading the tightrope
is hazardous.
I get tired of stripping away my skin
white fat showing
over stripy red of muscles pressed
onto paper.

I walk on emotions.
There's a trick to it,
I have to spread out discernment, tiptoe
toward what feels clean.
The sky, the sky
pulls.
Earth smashes.
My feelings are goldshot
as raku,
as easily breakable.

Feeling is the chasm that lures me
to the edge
makes me step off
again and again.

My weakness.
My great blazing skill.

The visions I accept as payment
for my proximity to the border
of falling,
that touch of air
along backs of my arms
as once again I edge onto the stretched rope.

I concentrate on the lit
warmth
    of the whole living creation,
    the pulse of ferns
    on a grey shale outcrop,
    the cool nose of a Siamese
    who loved me
    years before,
    even the breath
    of mountains.

Without this arc of flung perception
how else could I blunder my way through
ordinary kitchen magic,
the green transformations?
I cannot stop
pulling down
revelations.
I am a cook,
a woman trying to marry
sky to stew.
Why waste
what air gives
in such abundance:
the sun-edged flit of wings,
a red-winged blackbird
in flight?

I Want

*

Silence, or at least the red blare of need transformed to black.
Velvet black, the nap rubbed between us to flowers of purest
pleasure, white, tendrils graceful as vines in the closed room
uncoiling in slow motion.

*

Silver. For the planet to stop turning. To exist molten, clear of
all but the necessity of reach.

*

Pink. The urgency of mouths. A drop of oatmeal-smell I lick
off.

*

To lose myself. To know that somewhere I exist wordless and
absolute as a salamander. Slide of the moment into eternity,
taffy pulled and pulled into the green tide of surprise, the
spin of water, releasing me to the current, the overfall.

*

You. Now.

*

Transformation. The pull and ache of stone for the fire, white
snowflake crystals in granite for re-formation. The heart's fire,
where we sit of an evening, warming hands.
We scoop from possibility's barrel tiny stories which we shape
into perfect winged things. Release of the flutterers outside,
the blessing sign we sketch blue and definitive upon the
threshold.

*

To re-enter life free of need, breath no longer smoking white in the air. For the soft mouth of the world to accept me quick and beautiful as a cat in mid-air, claws extended. Not to be dangerous.

*

To be without past or future. Something other than a comet burning, consuming its own fiery tale.

Nail

I am a nail driven
into the side of morning,
darkening
as the metal smokes
and bubbles.
Truth's wild fire
is cleansing
or so I have been told.

(I wonder if that isn't a story told to young nails?)

The sun shows me grey
with zinc.

The morning is what drew me.
How could I resist the lure of clean beginnings
the rise of blue arcing above dense firs,
out to sea the shimmer
of light on water cauterizing?
The gold. The promise
I could be transformed.

I am sick
of longitudinal, how I seem made for one thing:
to pierce the burning wood of day.
I would be gold.
Here, in this place, I will hang in light
until I learn to rejoice
for the sharp reflections of water
a-glitter   on the face of the deep.

Become Water

Dry, dry, the white sheaves spin.

Become water,
the voice says. It is stern,
a black bear or a woman
grey hair past her elbows
whose hands rustle through the paper
of your days.

Learn river.
Behind you. How large
she is. Your shoulders hunch away
from her breath. She smells of change,
of ocean's edge.
She is glossy, she is clawed
and you don't dare turn,
for she would be wind,
gone,
leave you with no understanding
and with eyes bare.

Flow.
To what? From where?
From fern to sea and through
the holes in sky where light rushes
up from water,

meets the drift of stars,
sifts down to where
the grey clay bank shines
in the rain.
Cedar-water of you tumbling tea-coloured.
The quick green drops of maiden-hair fern
shiver
in the dedicated rush,
the passage.

I am the Long Breath Exhaled

I am clean laundry, then, think of me as its calm smell
Light of your home, see me burn at its centre, the
illumination, the clarity   I am lemon pound cake filling
up all the cracked corners of your old house with fragrance,
reassurance of something good, the child welcomed home
from school   I am the tick of the appointed time, the round
of cleaning done over, over, wiping of dust, polishing of wood,
the stain scrubbed from around the kitchen sink   The white
thankfulness at day's end

I am the relief when you open your eyes to see sunlight
through the curtains, its bounce from the neighbour's siding
I am the phone ringing with longed-for news   I am the
mother you always wanted, come to help out   I am the
morning jolt of water against your face, the tingle of your skin
afterward that says *clean*   I am lily-of-the-valley powder, the
twirled red petals of the dahlia you planted yesterday

I am the wind that takes distant cottonwoods and sets their
leaves fluttering like flags or children's hands at a parade   I
am the lustre of pearls, the spinning of cloud   I am the
splendid sway of sea lions; golden fur easing into abrupt dark
sea   I am the morning, this much I promise: you will not go
down into shadow without me   I am stillness at the core, the
long breath that says *safe*

Blue in this Country
is only Temporary

We think the old shapes of growth
are used up,
that a single crow cannot fly and be significant
against a mountain escarpment
its black shape seeming the same size
as the hazed green
that shoulders 1,500 feet
against the sun.
That's tired, people say despairingly.

We say this because soldiers shoot children
in Mexico.
We say this because the crow,
its scissoring of air, its belonging
to the horizontal plane of breath above us
does not acknowledge suffering.

We believe that potency has gone from old
myths, but no one has ever told the firs this.
Or Stellar's jays, those thieving
paradigms of blue,
or the northwesterly that sweeps up
afternoons   on this long lake chain.

The "we" who says this
is our stripped-of-magic selves
the we who believe in price tags
and the abandonment
of the old for some richer gratification.
New wives, new families, exotic myths
from some far country

made into sweat shirts
with gold and purple designs.

Can those without language be said to know?
Ask the wild strawberry and it will
feed you with red words.
Ask the rock
and it will show you sharp edges of young mountains
or palm-size rocks, grey and insignificant.
It will be up to you to solve
the *koan:* any one of the stones
was here before our ancestors had names.

Ask the sky what to believe
and it will tell you that blue in this country is only
temporary, that clouds are its soft vanity.
It will tell you silver falls down
mountains for years, that bears have green eyes
in the dark, it will confuse you
but belief has many answers.

Whether you accept them is another matter,

though it doesn't matter to the crow
who is in fact Crow, a solitary reflective shape
out of a black vast
handful of her kind,
or to the firs, who are one exultant form
with different trunks.

And the children? Place them in prayer
soft as wings, the comfort and clean smell of sky,
vast as Mountain with its roots going down
to prehistory or eternity where magma stirs slowly
says Hello

I may surprise you yet.

Maple

The big-leaf maple aloft
in the cloudless sky above Black Creek.
Its green bears the weight of summer
effortlessly, lit-up
with the fire of sap for the light
and swing of day.
(The secrecy of anchoring forest, shadows.
The dark reach of elderberry.
Prodigality of sword ferns.)

The maple makes use of light
in the only way it knows:
praise.
Praise for the hot sun on its leaves.
Praise for the tickle of breeze moist from
the creek.
Praise for the heaven of water,
its rush over rounded stones.
Praise for the maple's own tripod of roots, the slow
information of soil and crawlers; the wide
silvery tracks of slugs
that loop and return.
Praise for the sweetness of cottonwoods,
balsam an incense in the lavish air.
Praise for the grace of columbines.
Their colours.
Praise for purple, for nodding orange at the clearing's edge,
for the up-flung space
into which the maple's branches grow.

Flat on grassy earth, the observer,
straw hat half over eyes
is dizzy
with green hosannas.

The Green Woman

Days are repeated stars
of new green leaves.
I pray for clarity.
Outside the living room, Japanese maple leaves,
big-leaf maple leaves catch in my eyes.
I sit silent
wonder what I was doing
before the edge of colour on their points
had me tracing their shapes
beyond the window.

Oh, we keep a clean house.
The floor shines and I can turn from
leaves to find rest in the earthed red
of it, but outside the sky is rushing dizzily
north and I say to the wind
Where are you?
It is a cold friend
but constant.

At the swamp I throw sticks
our dog swims for and loses.
Doing so much planting
I am losing my language.
Mainly touch suffices; my fingers
curled round a root's tangled dialect,
the visitations of May foliage against sight;
osmanthus, mahonia with their holly-like prickles.
My garden plans anchored to the dust
with round stones, one white edge of paper lifting
to the breeze.

The dog's affectionate exuberance.
Muddy, her brow bone
against my face.

This spring I am the green woman.
I pray now
not to be overwhelmed.
All this life radiates out
and out
speechless from my earth-cracked hands.
I am dumb
with much birth.

Coming In and Going Out:
Pantoum

A poet is like a shaman, always falling off edges.
We come in, we go out holding onto longing
for something high and holy; burning bushes,
message-bearing doves are missives of power.

We come in, we go out holding onto longing
for knowledge of our connectedness with Light.
Message-bearing doves are missives of power
ecstatic beyond our limited senses.

For knowledge of our connectedness with Light
becomes joyful as feet running along a forest path
ecstatic beyond our limited senses
and the earth rises, springy, a skin for some great good,

becomes joyful as feet running along a forest path
while the mind shuffles words, notices exact textures
and the earth rises, springy, a skin for some great good
that radiates through the woodland duff, the fallen fir boughs.

While the mind shuffles words, notices exact textures
the poet processes tea-coloured cedar-water
that radiates through the woodland duff, the fallen fir boughs,
through one eye; with the other knows the forest a benediction.

The poet processes tea-coloured cedar-water
through the prayer she makes for her daughter
through one eye; with the other knows the forest a benediction.
and is lost between the shaman and the Word.

Through the prayer she makes for her daughter,
the poet pauses at an uprooted cedar, a huge orange starfish,
and is lost between the shaman and the Word;
a reflecting pool where the cedar was torn from earth.

The poet pauses at an uprooted cedar, a huge orange starfish.
A litany of ferns is luminous in the January mist.
A reflecting pool where the cedar was torn from earth
the shaman's reminder that beneath lies spiritual strength.

A litany of ferns is luminous in the January mist.
Tiny, green, they droop with such grace;
the shaman's reminder that beneath lies spiritual strength.
Today she yields to creation, the warmth of its waves.

Tiny, green, they droop with such grace
the sweet spaces between trees are full.
Today she yields to creation, the warmth of its waves.
We come in, we go out holding onto longing

to understand the lapping certainty of safety,
for something high and holy, burning bushes.
We come in, we go out holding onto longing.
A poet is like a shaman, always falling off edges.

After Comes the Ambulance Ride

I'm dying, you know that?
my father says conversationally.
He is seventy-five.
Prayer is the small comforts of candles,
the lemon tang of herb tea.
Prayer is continuing to reach out with thoughts
pocked with salt
fierce indentations thrown onto packed snow
that spread and clear the pavement to dry white
like withered skin.

> *The mortality rate for us all*
> *is the same,* my doctor Kirsten says,
> *one hundred percent.*

Prayer is resisting the continual engulfing of fear,
looking around for something to praise.
Lamplight slants down on a bare desk
carries with it a corollary of summer:
this is
so what was once,
is still true, goes on somewhere
in that hazed country of memory;
white pines
throw the delirious tang of their resin
into the softness of August.
Each branch spare and perfect
as a Japanese screen.
Heat wilted us then, helianthemums at midday,
golden, longing for water.

Now it is February.
Night is the hardest time.
My father sleeps now, struggles for air.
Daily he slides toward
a line where the winter river meets sky
and his doctor will not come, will not call back.
I grope for comfort
toward light,
try to poise my weight
so I can pray with the radiant effectiveness
of an anchorite.

Peace is the most continuing of prayers.
Slip-sliding away, my father calls it and I feel
as he does each seismic tilt
toward the fault where he will fall
and I be left behind.

This afternoon he sat in the kitchen across
the scrubbed pine table,
breath whistling in his chest, and said
All last night I dreamed I couldn't breathe.
And I kept waking up and it was true, I couldn't.
Then I didn't know if I was awake or not.
For answer, all I could do was
top up my father's tea.
Earlier when he tried to lift the one-cup pot
he had poured scalding tea all over his leg.
I'm fine. It doesn't hurt.
The bare leg sticking out
from his white terry dressing gown
glanced at as if it belonged to someone
far away. His concern a handful of aerosol puffers,
green handle, orange handle, blue handle:

sympathetic magics, medications sucked deep
into the throat.
The tea cup steamed.
My father politely refused the minestrone
I had spent the afternoon making. *It smells delicious
but I can't eat.*

Tonight my heart is a scallop shell,
a giant one, hollowed to hold
the words we have given
one another this visit, principally
I love you,
Thanks and *You're welcome.*
It's shorthand for everything.
What it comes down to
in the end
the every-day courtesies of our lives
drawn up, a blanket,
to warm this dying.

Fishers of Poems

A pond, silver.
The time is dusk or early
morning, the light uncertain between
the opening of day
and the dark energy of night.

Our belts clink and tinkle, metal
against metal. Barbless hooks.

Out in the water, poems are feeding,
their heads raised to catch the glitter
of stars. We move now into the season of
Crab, faintest of all constellations.

White glow against the black bowed sky.

There are more poems than hooks.
Perhaps not more than stars
but the pond is stream-fed and all year
the fins of radiant newcomers can be seen
making their purposeful way up to where
water widens and stills.

And we wait.
We listen for the one whisper
that confirms what we know or fear.
Watch for the colour that cracks our heart
neatly as a brown egg, halved.

What words will we hoist from the wet
and take gleaming home?

Mother of Lights

1. A DIFFERENT WORLD

No shadows
of turning, sharp angles of dark moving
where you gasp, burdened
in the chill thinness of moonlight.
None of that prowling aura
that says a big cat might be lurking
dangerous outside bedroom windows.
Around here, it happens a few times every year:
a cougar runs away
with the family dog
dangling from its mouth.

No night.

Unchanging substantiality rises up to greet you
through the ripped seam of the cosmos,
leaking light all the way.
You look at moss and laugh
because it is not only the green damp
of miniature ferns
but creation, dealing grace even to
the infinitesimal.

2. SHELTERING OF WONDERS

You hoped, when you were a teenager,
to use books to get to a place
where hurt
could not find you
anymore:
a realm of fire-lit rooms,
the clean tang of herbs, drying,
a library where each volume
was not only a pass to marvels
but safety.

Instead you learned to live with pain —
every kind —
as if it were a loop
of tungsten worn through the lungs.
Incandescent perhaps,
but crippling.
With books there was always an end;
you shut them and had to breathe again.

Pain, fear, they are the same names
for the weight of earth.
The place where nothing works
but the catch of breath,
the shiver as you struggle
to inhale enough richness to go on.
Your hands reach for walls, a wood door frame
to steady yourself. Something
to catch hold of.

3. SUN OF HEALING

It's not that you've forgotten light
pouring through matter, the trick
is to remember the swing,
weightless and unobstructed
through solid air.
You become vertical, porous
take in the good that you perceive sometimes
through your skin,
fragrant as fresh-picked basil or pennyroyal.

The visible is just a shadow of this
for all its trees and the brown anxious eyes
of a dog who loves you.
The good night hugs of children,
breath sweet on your cheek.

What we see is the rind on a tangerine.
We are after the juice,
the fine spray of aromatic oils
as fingernails peel away
the inessential.

And it means giving up pain.
Not a forgetting, but a seeing
through.
A discarding.
It is hard to abandon the familiar,
the tearing whistle when you push air
in and out, that hurt you feel married to
it's been with you so long.
But it is time.

Time to drop to that steady
place beneath the green verticals of evergreens
where peace, an unseen river, rises.
The dog looks at you with the love
you see now is from the unseen sun
of healing.
Children play here, whole.

Light is your home.
In its clarity, you renounce isolation
and its sad illusions.
Joyous, you breathe in
as much as you want, let the rest
of the world, re-discovered,
wash over you.

ABOUT THE AUTHOR

Zoë Landale was born in Toronto but has lived most of her life in British Columbia. When she was seventeen, she went commercial salmon fishing. The seven seasons she spent on the water have affected her writing profoundly. When her daughter started kindergarten, she went to the University of British Columbia and resumed her studies, graduating in 1995 with a MFA in Creative Writing.

Landale has published four previous books, one of non-fiction, two of poetry, and a novel. Her poetry and prose have been published in major literary magazines from coast to coast as well as in mass market magazines such as *Reader's Digest, Canadian Living, Chatelaine* and *Harrowsmith.* Her work has appeared in several dozen anthologies in Canada and the US and has won significant awards in three genres — fiction, poetry and non-fiction — including a National Magazine Gold.

As well as working as a freelance writer and editor, Landale has also worked as a garden designer and teaches Creative Writing through Continuing Education at North Island College in Courtenay. She lives with her husband Garnet Coburn, daughter Jocelyne Coburn, and assorted animals in a house they built themselves in the Comox Valley, on Vancouver Island.